GRAPHIC SCIENCE

THE EARTH-SHAKING FACTS ABOUT

EARTHQUAKES

WITH **MAX AXIOM**
SUPER SCIENTIST

by Katherine Krohn

illustrated by Tod Smith and Al Milgrom

Consultant:
Professor Kenneth H. Rubin
Department of Geology and Geophysics
School of Ocean and Earth Science and Technology
University of Hawaii, Honolulu

Capstone press

Mankato, Minnesota

Graphic Library is published by Capstone Press,
151 Good Counsel Drive, P.O. Box 669, Mankato, Minnesota 56002.
www.capstonepress.com

Printed in the United States of America

1 2 3 4 5 6 13 12 11 10 09 08

Library of Congress Cataloging-in-Publication Data
Krohn, Katherine E.
The Earth-shaking facts about earthquakes with Max Axiom, super scientist / by Katherine Krohn ; illustrated by Tod Smith and Al Milgrom.
p. cm. — (Graphic library. Graphic science)
Summary: "In graphic novel format, follows the adventures of Max Axiom as he explains the science behind earthquakes"— Provided by publisher.
Includes bibliographical references and index.
ISBN-13: 978-1-4296-1328-6 (hardcover)
ISBN-10: 1-4296-1328-9 (hardcover)
ISBN-13: 978-1-4296-1759-8 (softcover pbk.)
ISBN-10: 1-4296-1759-4 (softcover pbk.)
1. Earthquakes — Juvenile literature. I. Smith, Tod, ill. II. Milgrom, Al III. Title. IV. Series.
QE521.3.K76 2008
551.22 — dc22 2007025091

Art Director and Designer
Bob Lentz

Cover Artist
Tod Smith

Colorist
Krista Ward

Editor
Christine Peterson

Photo illustration credit
Shutterstock/Sean Gladwell, 24 (map)

TABLE OF CONTENTS

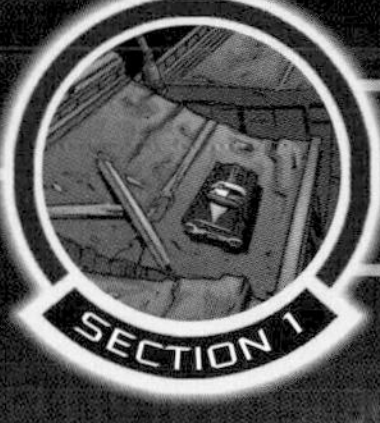
SECTION 1

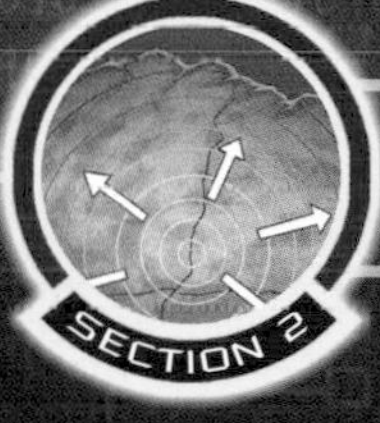
SECTION 2

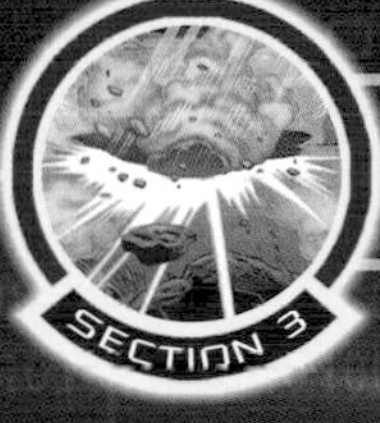
SECTION 3

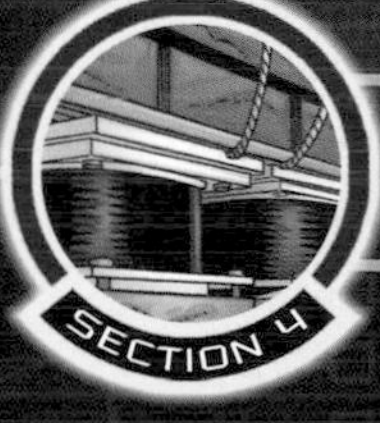
SECTION 4

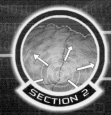

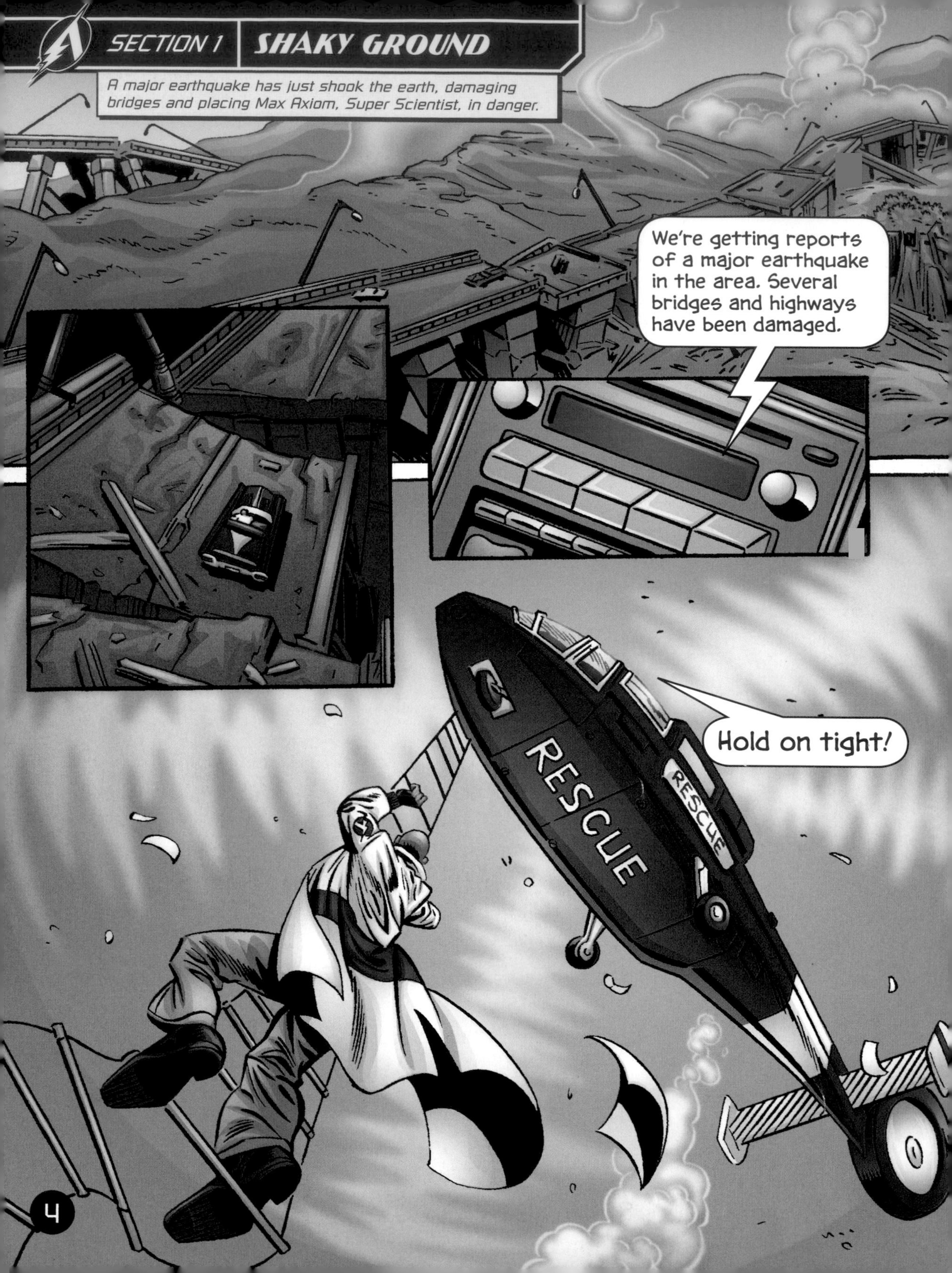
SECTION 1 SHAKY GROUND
A major earthquake has just shook the earth, damaging bridges and placing Max Axiom, Super Scientist, in danger.
We're getting reports of a major earthquake in the area. Several bridges and highways have been damaged.
RESCUE
RESCUE
Hold on tight!

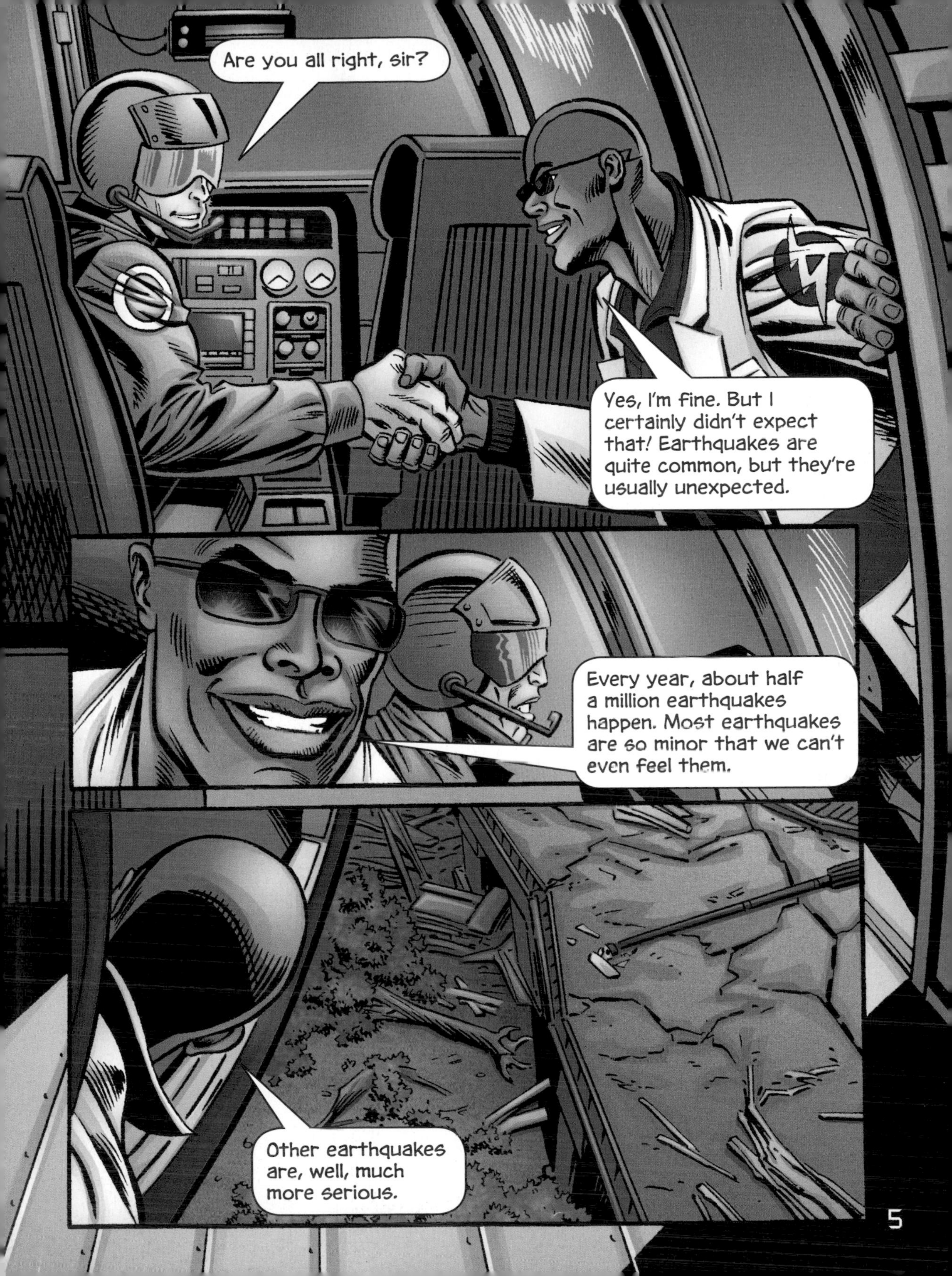
Are you all right, sir?
Yes, I'm fine. But I certainly didn't expect that! Earthquakes are quite common, but they're usually unexpected.
Every year, about half a million earthquakes happen. Most earthquakes are so minor that we can't even feel them.
Other earthquakes are, well, much more serious.

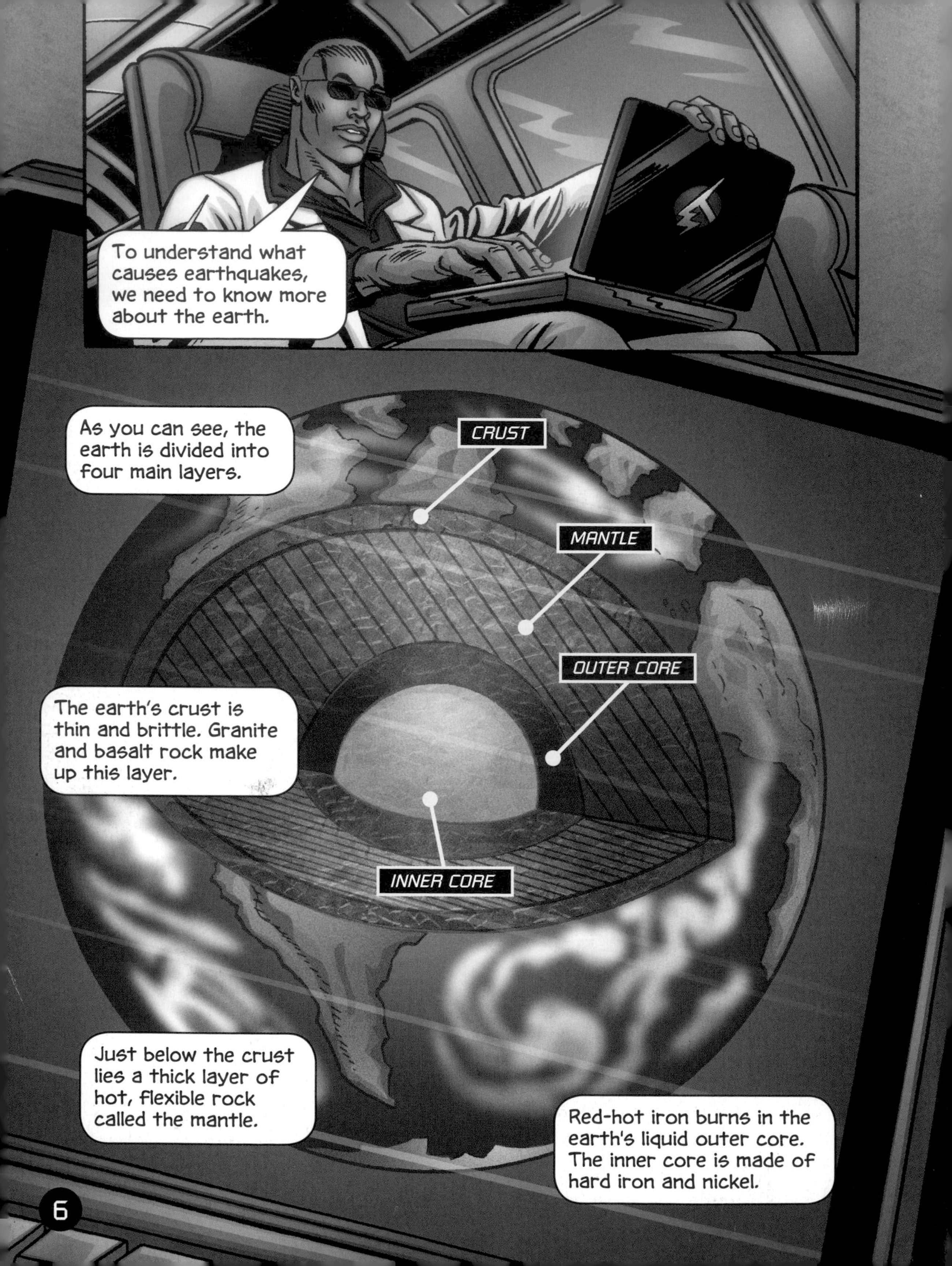
To understand what causes earthquakes, we need to know more about the earth.
As you can see, the earth is divided into four main layers.
CRUST
MANTLE
OUTER CORE
INNER CORE
The earth's crust is thin and brittle. Granite and basalt rock make up this layer.
Just below the crust lies a thick layer of hot, flexible rock called the mantle.
Red-hot iron burns in the earth's liquid outer core. The inner core is made of hard iron and nickel.

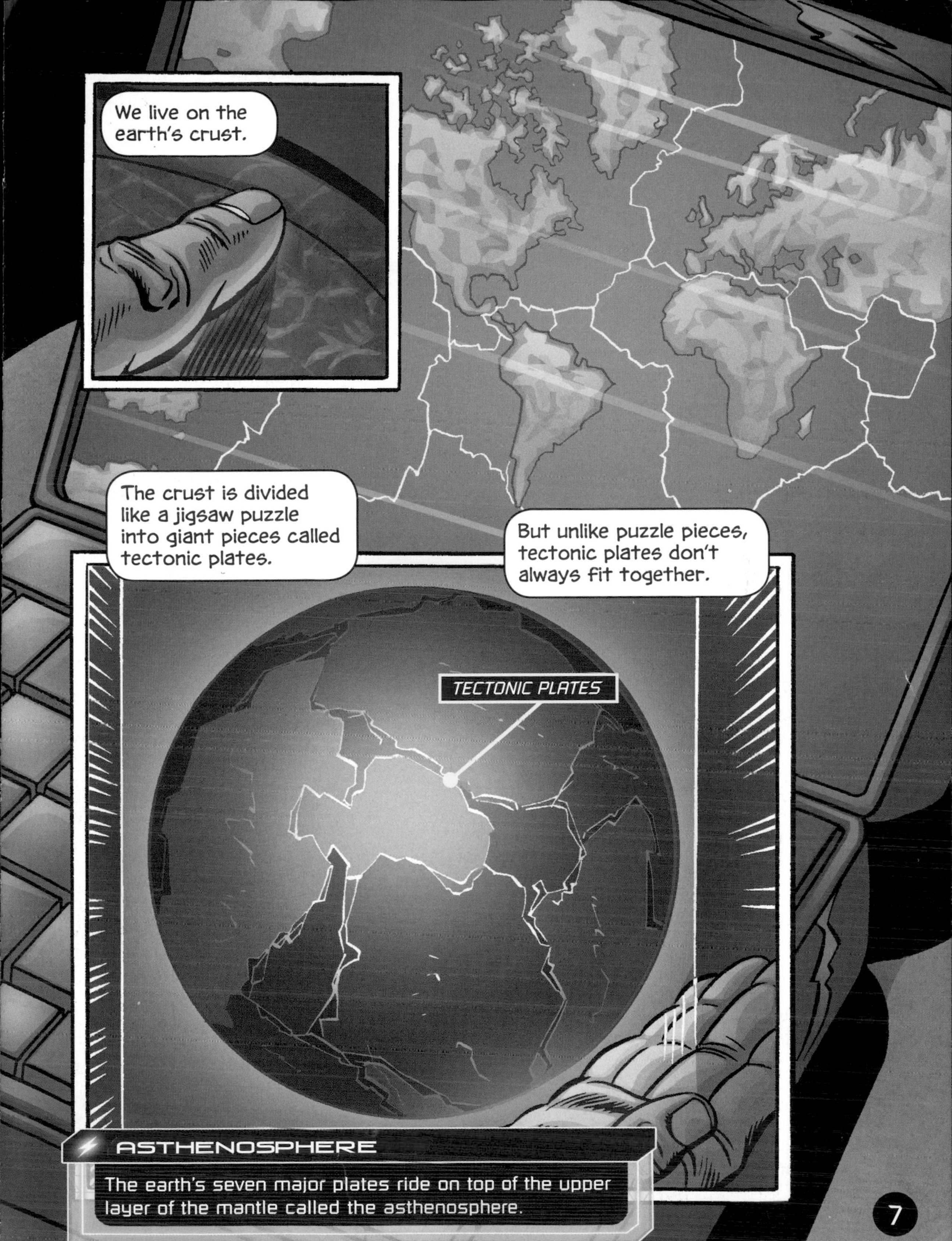

We live on the earth's crust.
The crust is divided like a jigsaw puzzle into giant pieces called tectonic plates.
But unlike puzzle pieces, tectonic plates don't always fit together.
TECTONIC PLATES
ASTHENOSPHERE
The earth's seven major plates ride on top of the upper layer of the mantle called the asthenosphere.

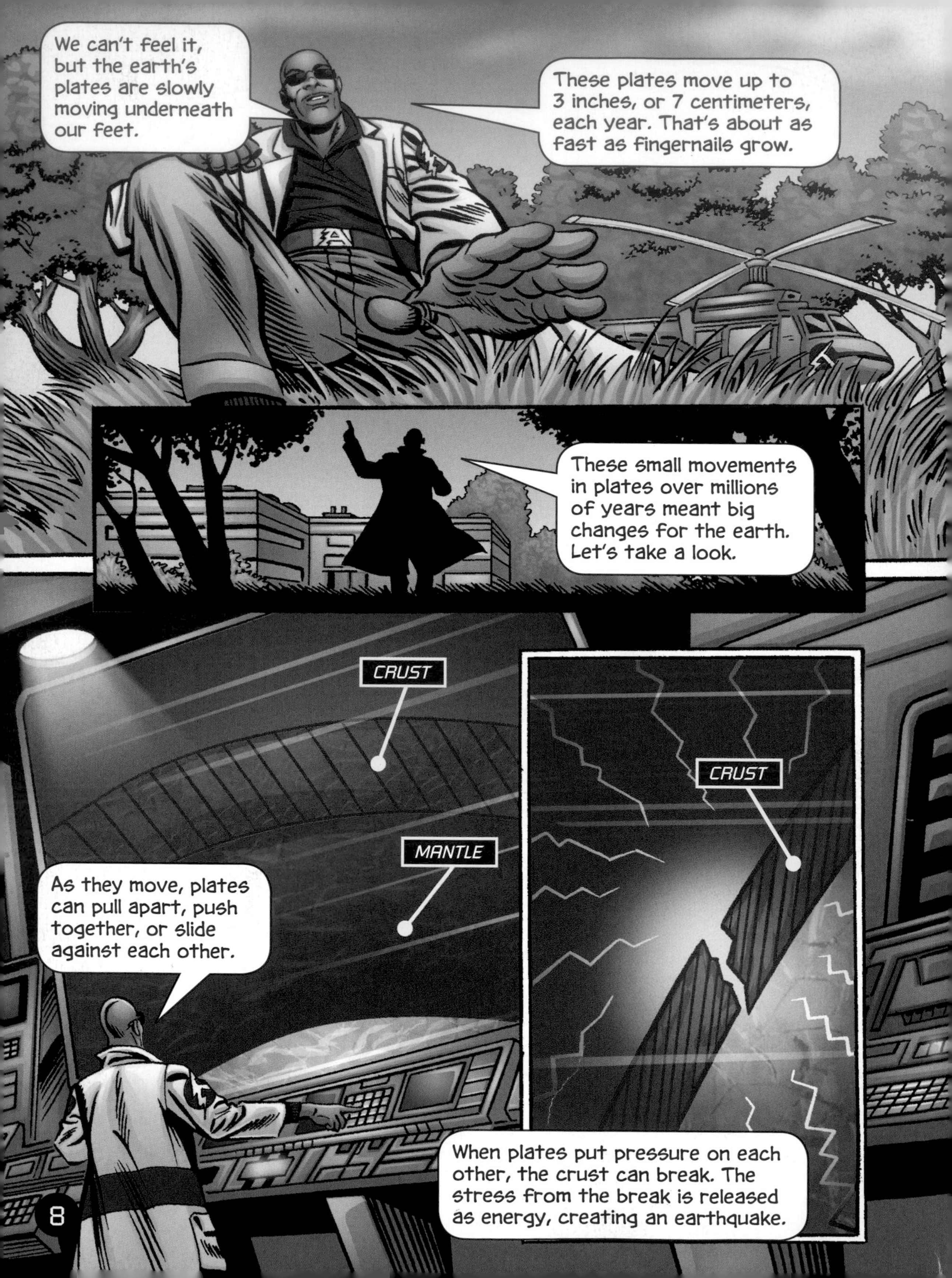
We can't feel it, but the earth's plates are slowly moving underneath our feet.
These plates move up to 3 inches, or 7 centimeters, each year. That's about as fast as fingernails grow.
These small movements in plates over millions of years meant big changes for the earth. Let's take a look.
CRUST
MANTLE
As they move, plates can pull apart, push together, or slide against each other.
CRUST
When plates put pressure on each other, the crust can break. The stress from the break is released as energy, creating an earthquake.

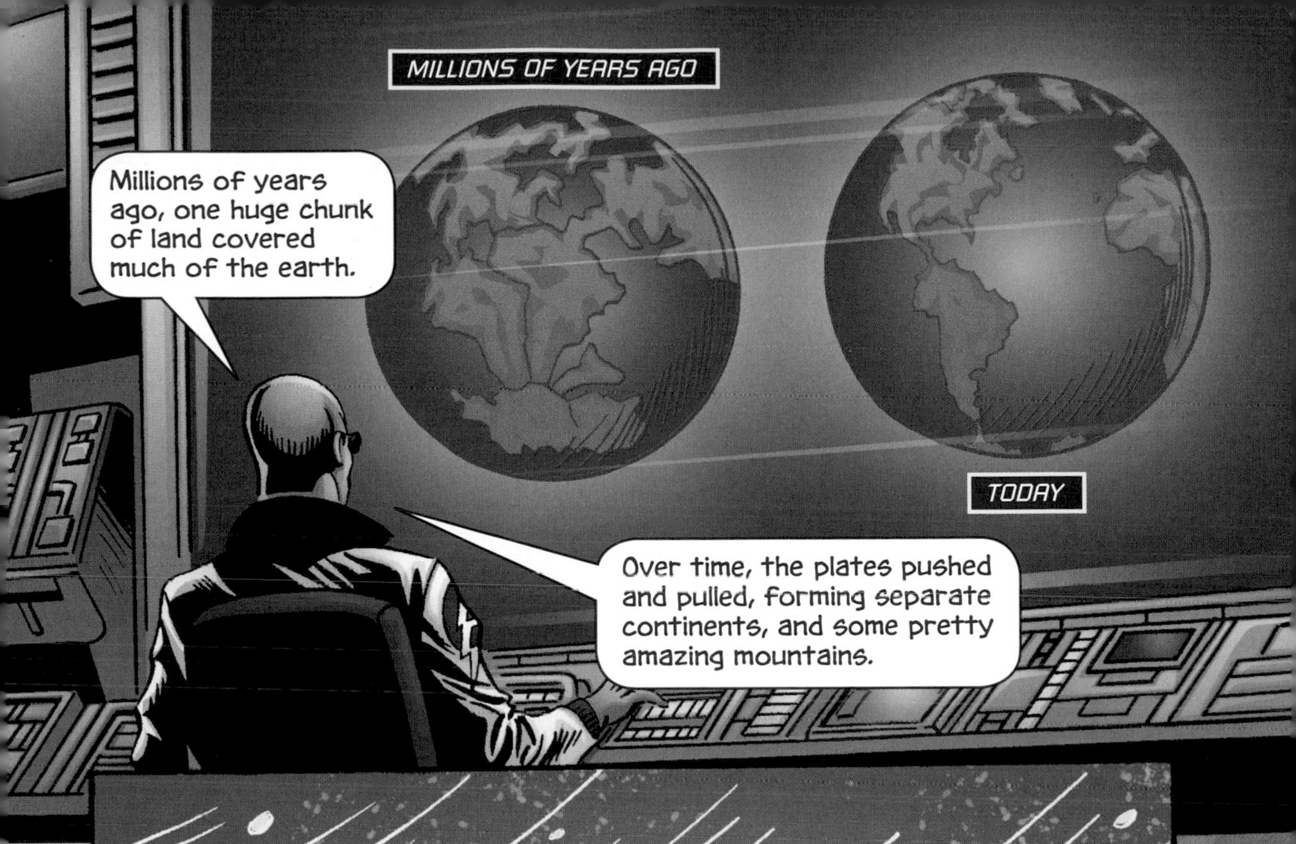
MILLIONS OF YEARS AGO
Millions of years ago, one huge chunk of land covered much of the earth.
TODAY
Over time, the plates pushed and pulled, forming separate continents, and some pretty amazing mountains.

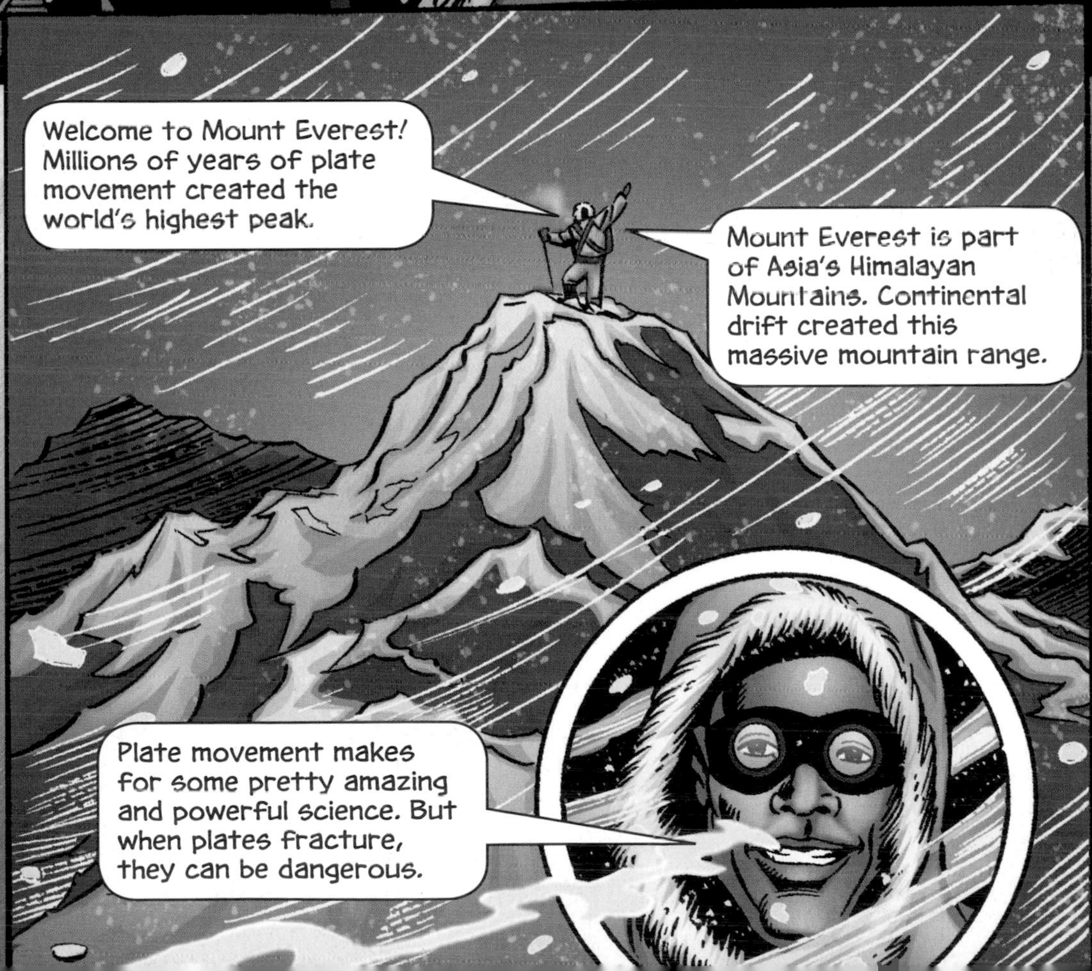
Welcome to Mount Everest! Millions of years of plate movement created the world's highest peak.
Mount Everest is part of Asia's Himalayan Mountains. Continental drift created this massive mountain range.
Plate movement makes for some pretty amazing and powerful science. But when plates fracture, they can be dangerous.

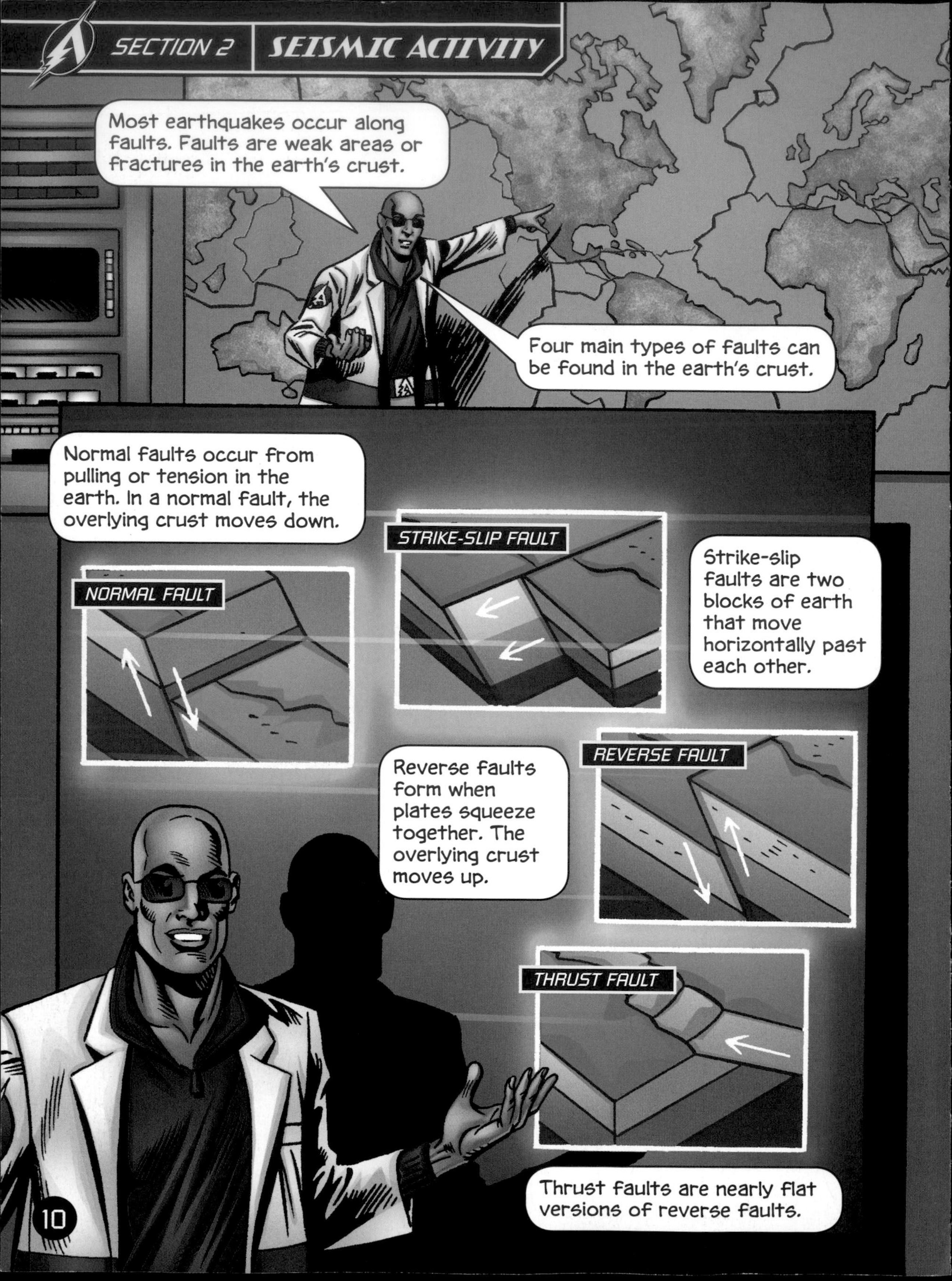
Most earthquakes occur along faults. Faults are weak areas or fractures in the earth's crust.
Four main types of faults can be found in the earth's crust.
Normal faults occur from pulling or tension in the earth. In a normal fault, the overlying crust moves down.
NORMAL FAULT
STRIKE-SLIP FAULT
Strike-slip faults are two blocks of earth that move horizontally past each other.
Reverse faults form when plates squeeze together. The overlying crust moves up.
REVERSE FAULT
THRUST FAULT
Thrust faults are nearly flat versions of reverse faults.

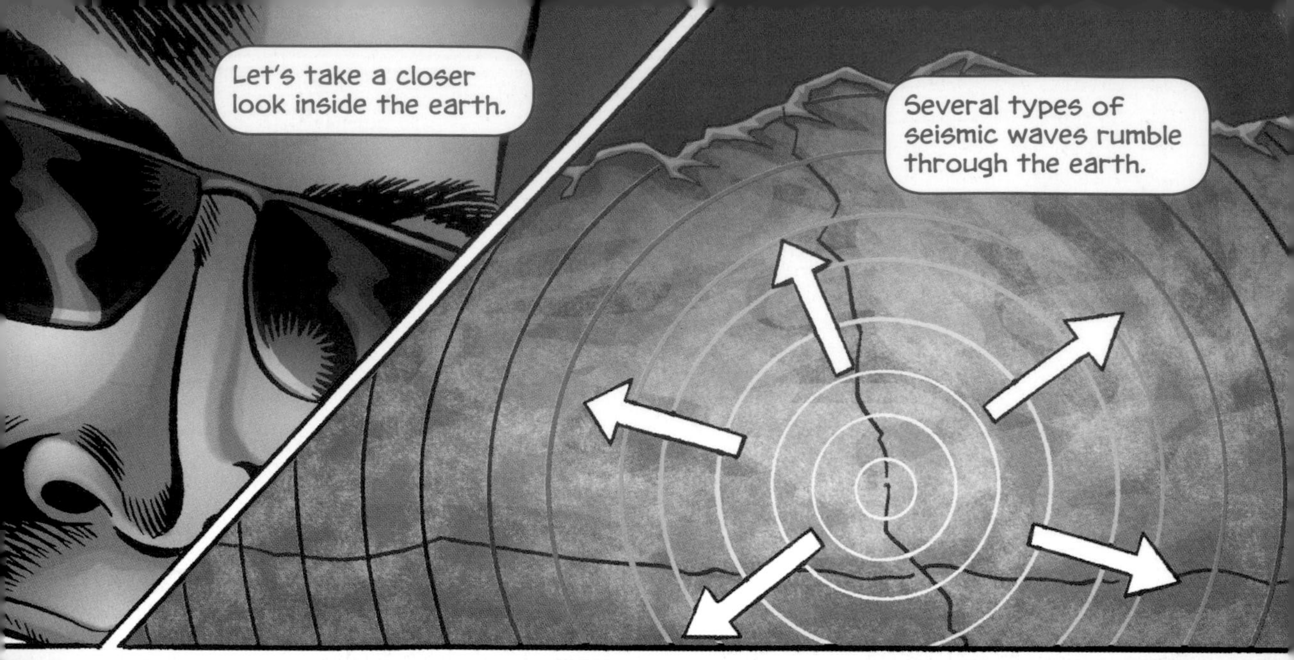
Let's take a closer look inside the earth.
Several types of seismic waves rumble through the earth.

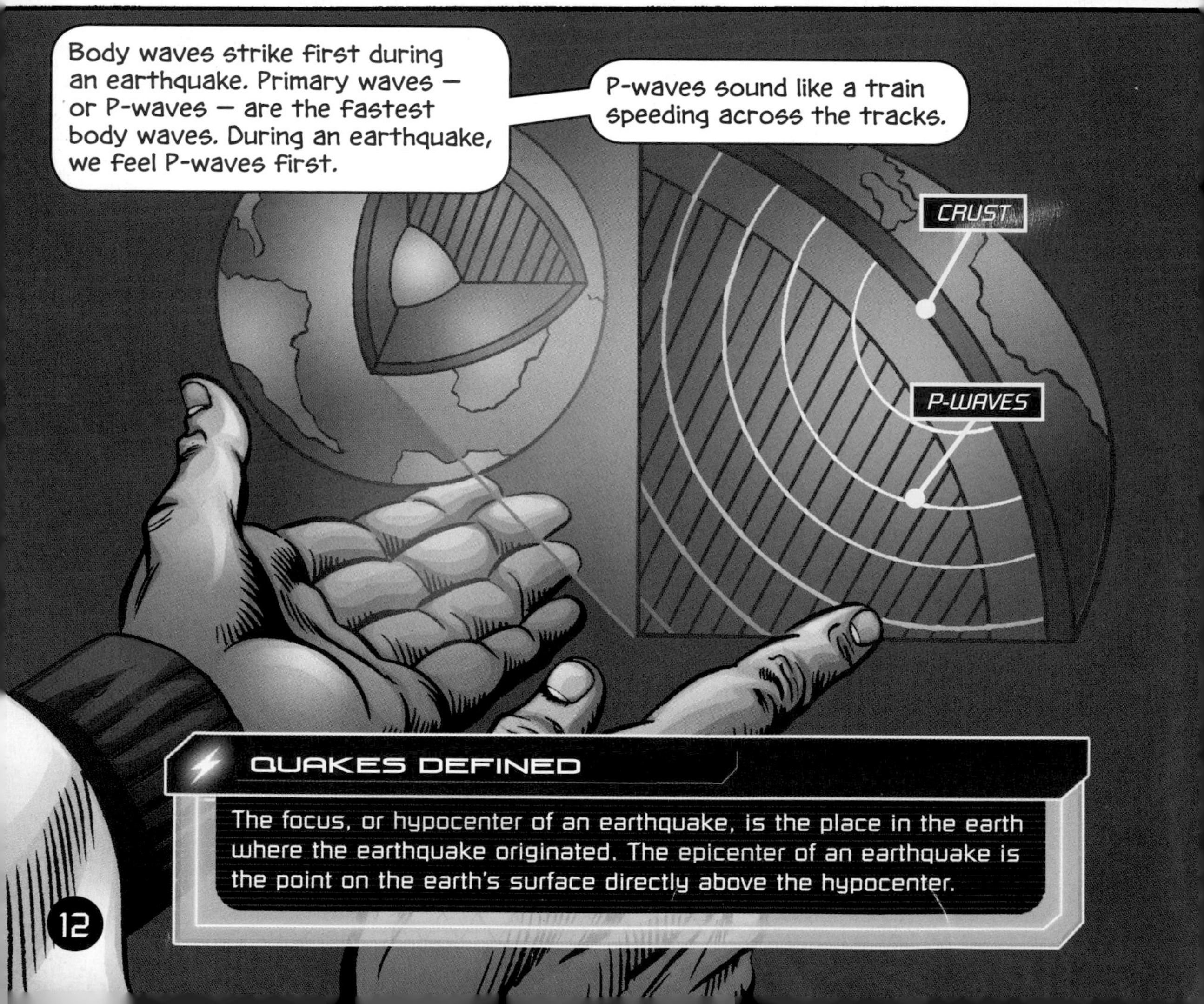
Body waves strike first during an earthquake. Primary waves — or P-waves — are the fastest body waves. During an earthquake, we feel P-waves first.
P-waves sound like a train speeding across the tracks.
CRUST
P-WAVES

QUAKES DEFINED

The focus, or hypocenter of an earthquake, is the place in the earth where the earthquake originated. The epicenter of an earthquake is the point on the earth's surface directly above the hypocenter.

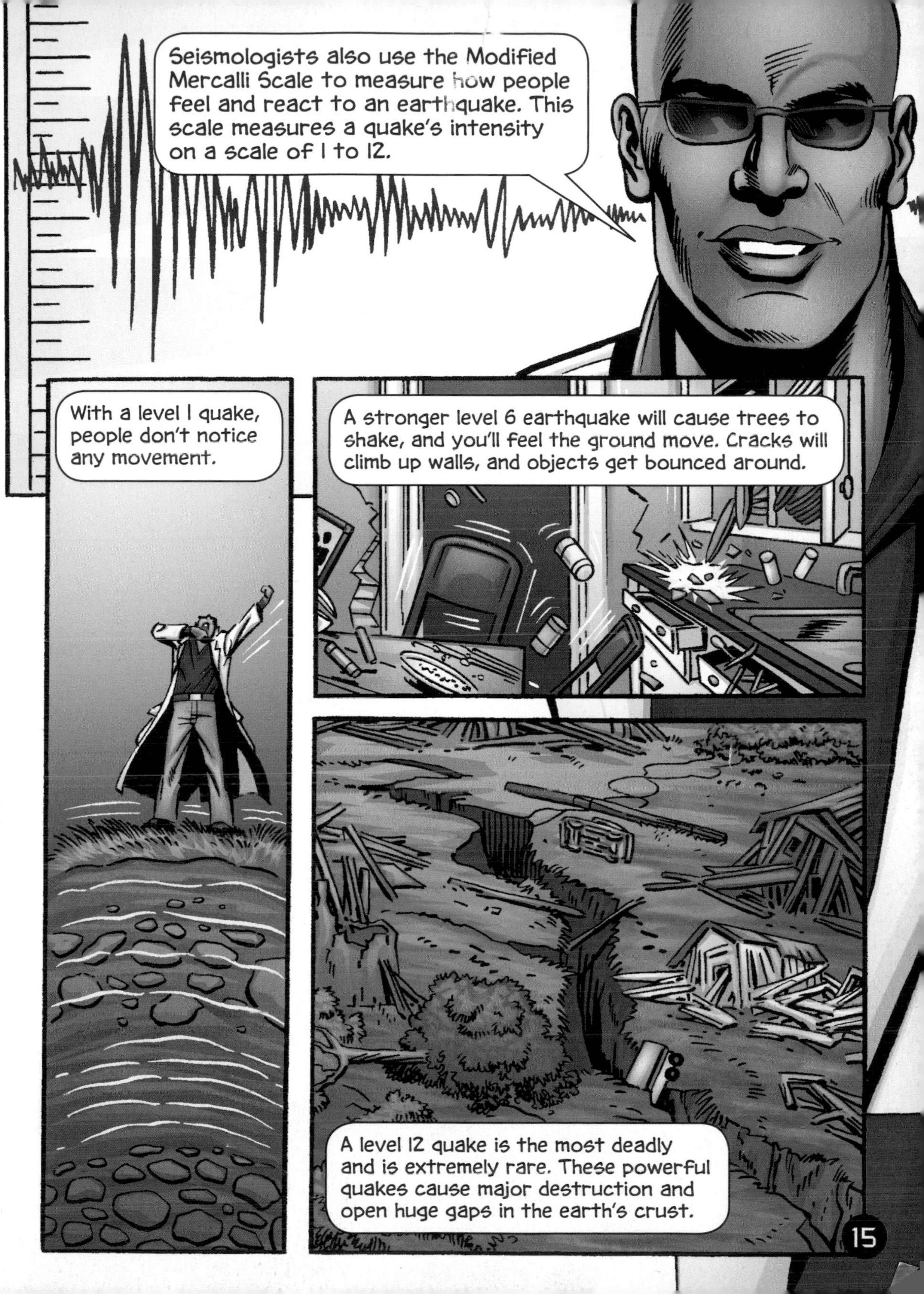
Seismologists also use the Modified Mercalli Scale to measure how people feel and react to an earthquake. This scale measures a quake's intensity on a scale of 1 to 12.
With a level 1 quake, people don't notice any movement.
A stronger level 6 earthquake will cause trees to shake, and you'll feel the ground move. Cracks will climb up walls, and objects get bounced around.
A level 12 quake is the most deadly and is extremely rare. These powerful quakes cause major destruction and open huge gaps in the earth's crust.

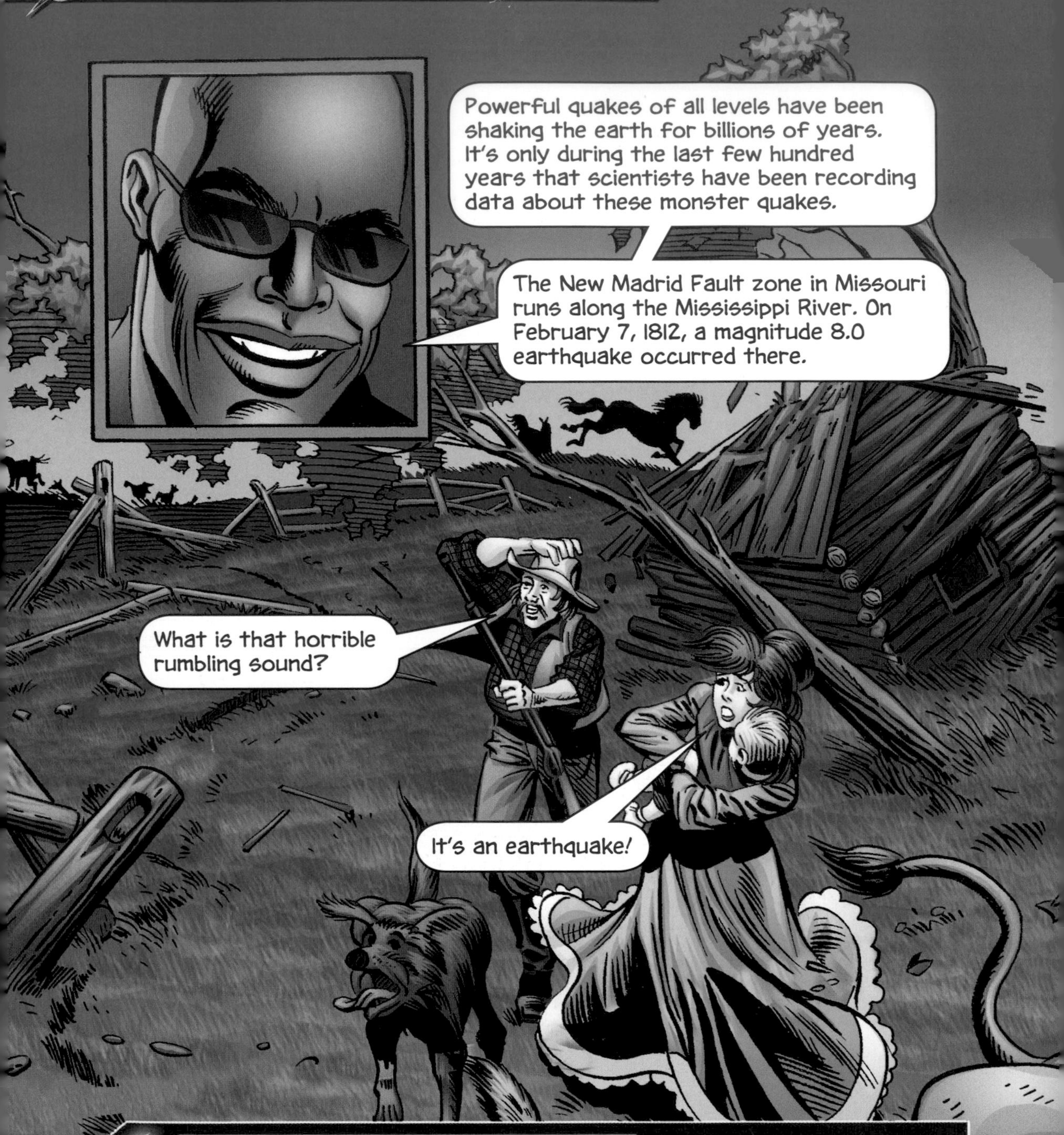
Powerful quakes of all levels have been shaking the earth for billions of years. It's only during the last few hundred years that scientists have been recording data about these monster quakes.
The New Madrid Fault zone in Missouri runs along the Mississippi River. On February 7, 1812, a magnitude 8.0 earthquake occurred there.
What is that horrible rumbling sound?
It's an earthquake!

SHOCKS

Smaller earthquakes that happen before a large quake are called foreshocks. The highest magnitude earthquake is called the mainshock. An aftershock is a smaller earthquake that follows the mainshock.

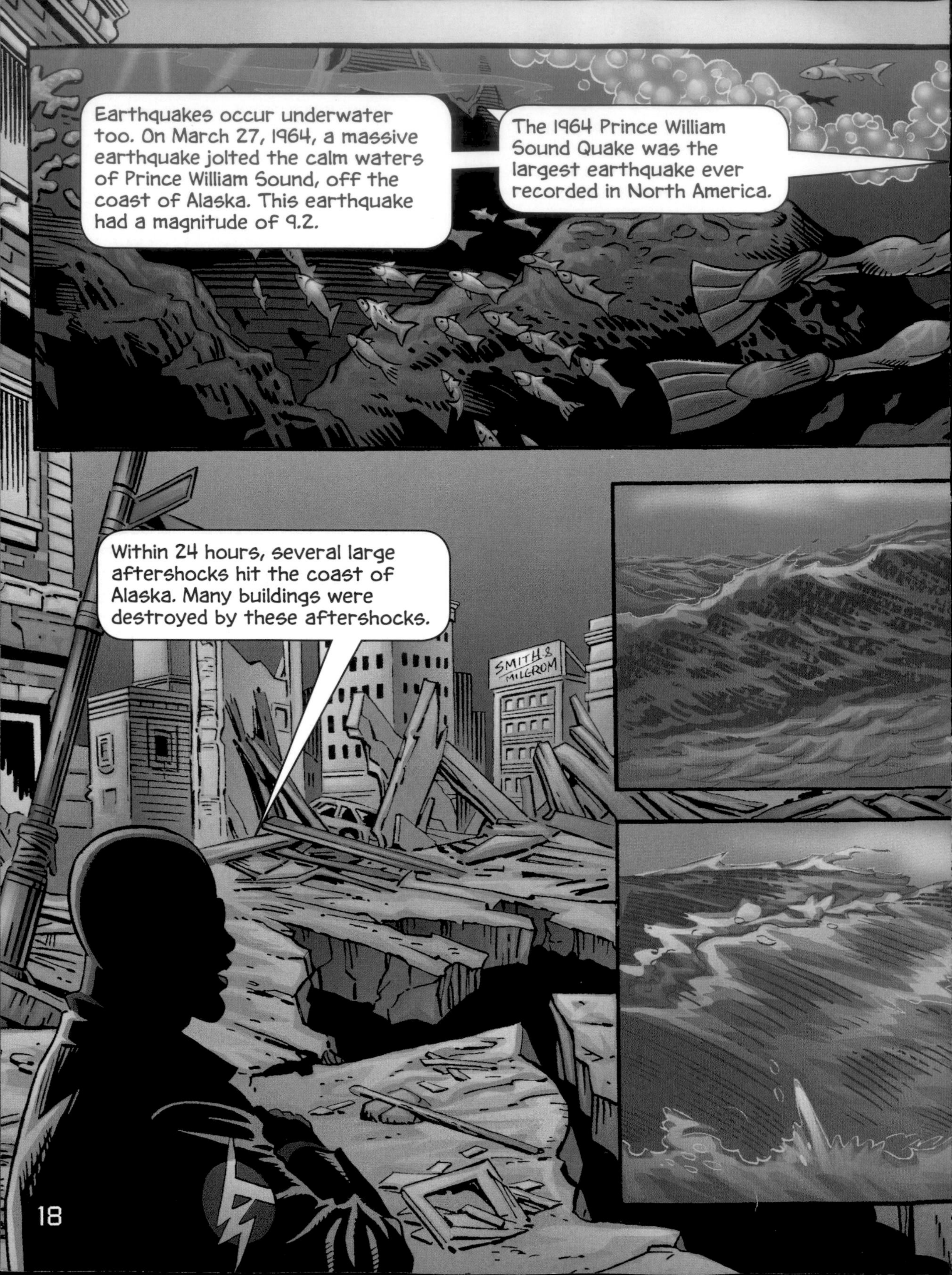
Earthquakes occur underwater too. On March 27, 1964, a massive earthquake jolted the calm waters of Prince William Sound, off the coast of Alaska. This earthquake had a magnitude of 9.2.
The 1964 Prince William Sound Quake was the largest earthquake ever recorded in North America.
Within 24 hours, several large aftershocks hit the coast of Alaska. Many buildings were destroyed by these aftershocks.
SMITH & MILGROM

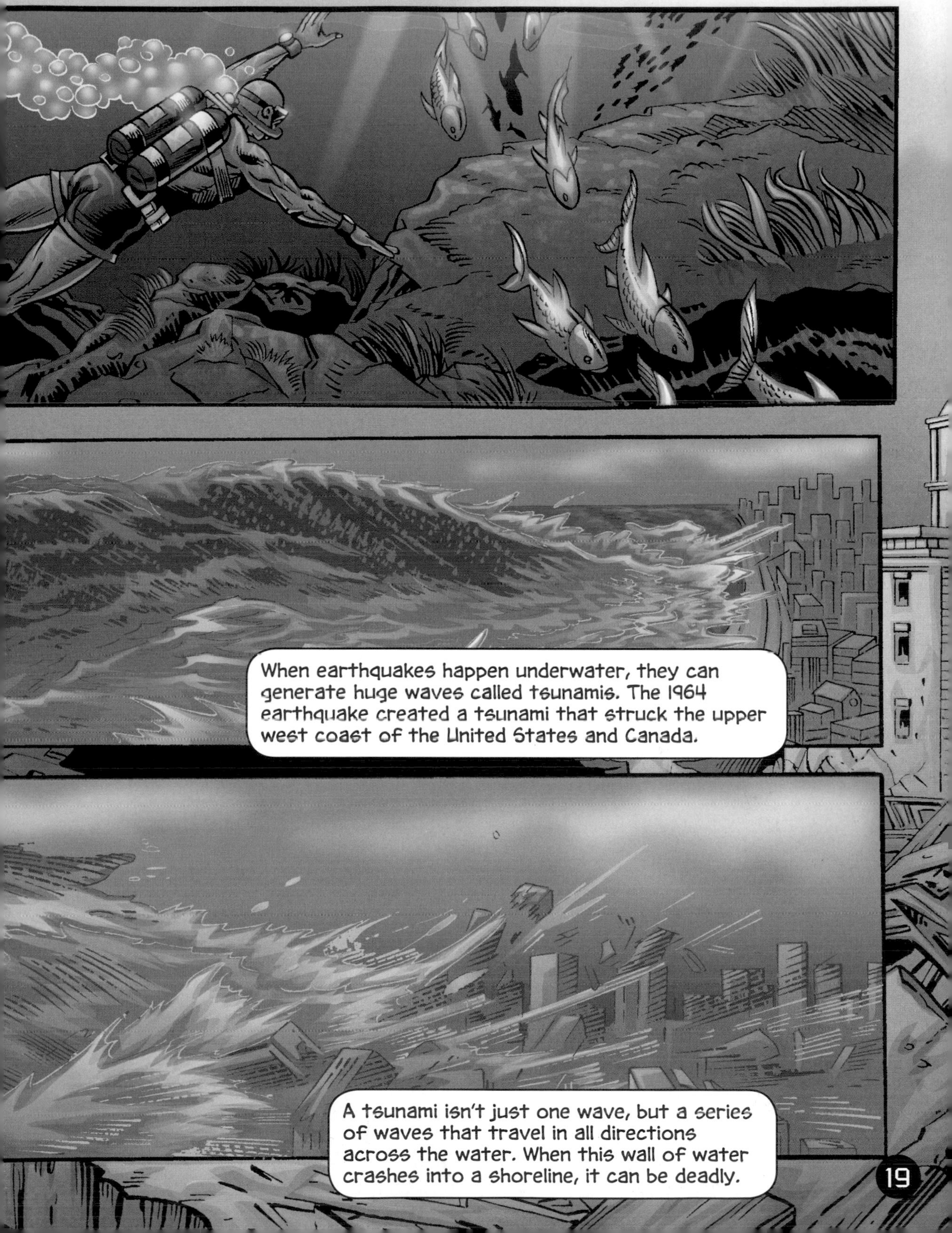
When earthquakes happen underwater, they can generate huge waves called tsunamis. The 1964 earthquake created a tsunami that struck the upper west coast of the United States and Canada.
A tsunami isn't just one wave, but a series of waves that travel in all directions across the water. When this wall of water crashes into a shoreline, it can be deadly.

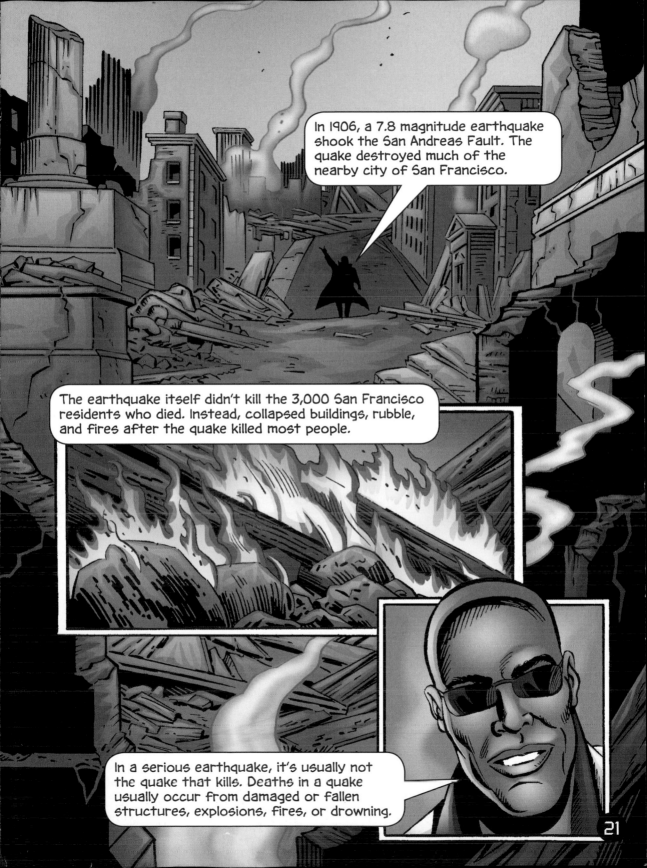

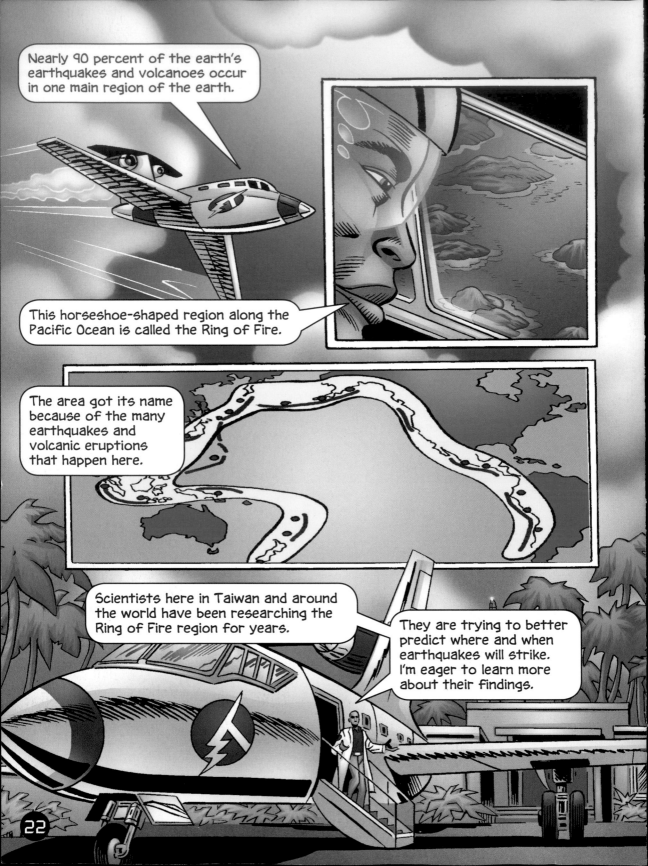

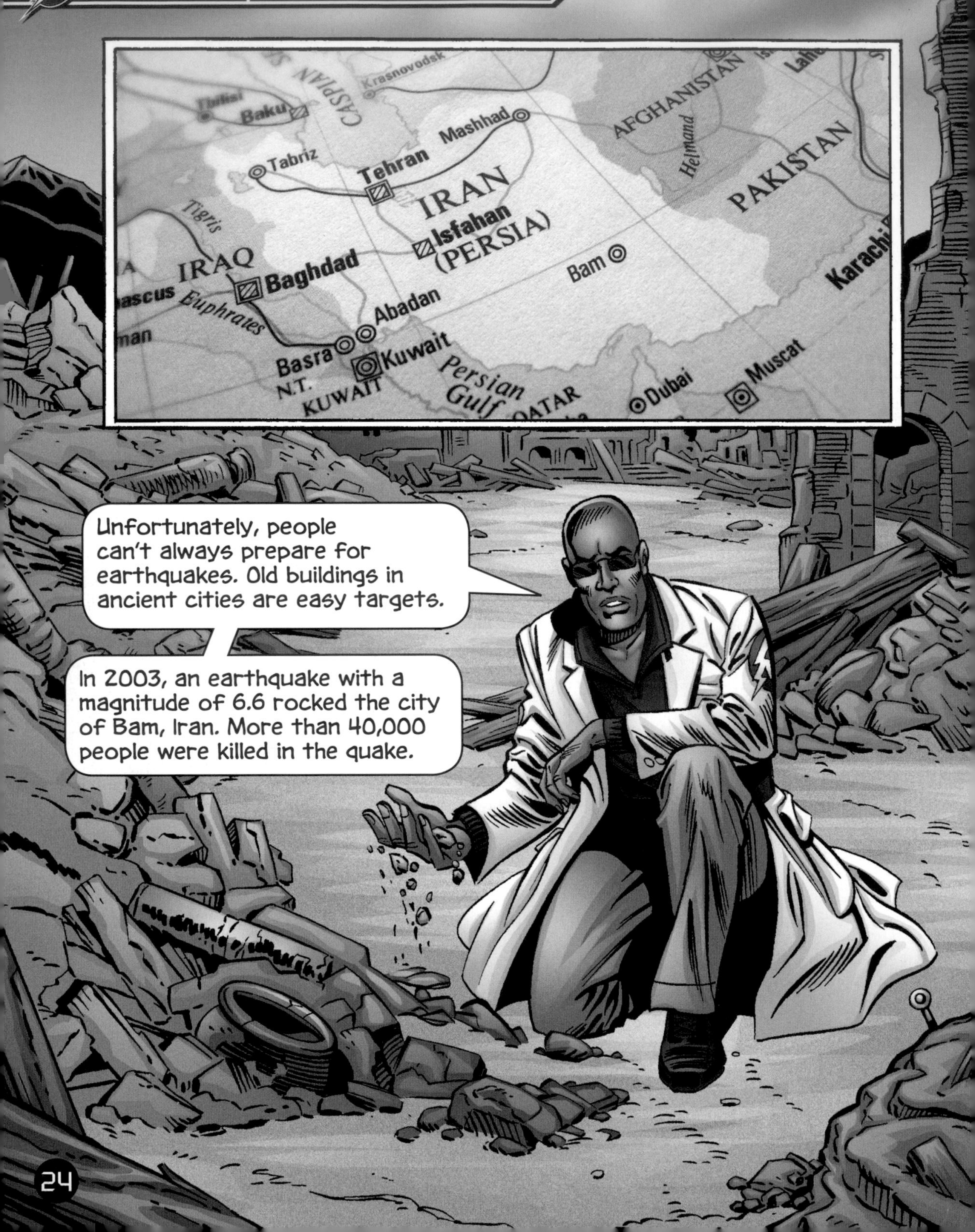
Krasnovodsk
CASPIAN
Baku
Tbilisi
Mashhad
Tabriz
Tehran
IRAN
Isfahan
(PERSIA)
AFGHANISTAN
Helmand
PAKISTAN
Tigris
IRAQ
Baghdad
Bam
Karachi
Euphrates
Abadan
Basra
Kuwait
N.T.
KUWAIT
Persian
Gulf
QATAR
Dubai
Muscat
Unfortunately, people can't always prepare for earthquakes. Old buildings in ancient cities are easy targets.
In 2003, an earthquake with a magnitude of 6.6 rocked the city of Bam, Iran. More than 40,000 people were killed in the quake.

MORE ABOUT EARTHQUAKES

About 500,000 earthquakes are detected by seismologists in the world each year. Of these earthquakes, only about 100,000 of those can be felt. Only about 100 earthquakes each year cause damage.

Scientists have learned that the crustal plate of India collided with the crust of Asia to form the Himalayan Mountains. Scientists believe these mountains are still pushing together and slowly rising.

The largest earthquake of the 20th century occurred in Chile on May 22, 1960. This quake registered 9.5 on the Richter scale. The greatest number of people killed in one earthquake was in China in 1556. The quake killed about 830,000 people.

Tsunami waves can be far-reaching and deadly. Waves from the 1964 Alaska earthquake struck many towns in the Prince William Sound area of Alaska and along the Gulf of Alaska. These waves killed 21 people in Alaska.

Caused by earthquakes, volcanic eruptions, or landslides, tsunamis can travel at speeds up to 600 miles (966 kilometers) per hour.

Researchers in Buffalo, New York, discovered that rubber pads placed under earthquake-resistant buildings can cut the force of a quake by 25 percent.

Geologist A. C. Lawson named the San Andreas Fault in 1895. He named it after the San Andreas Lake, located on the fault, about 20 miles (32 kilometers) south of San Francisco.

 Plate movement along the San Andreas Fault created many mountainous areas. Scientists have studied the Transverse Range segment the most.

 Southern California has about 10,000 earthquakes each year. North Dakota and Florida have had the fewest number of earthquakes in the United States.

MORE ABOUT

SUPER SCIENTIST

Real name: Maxwell J. Axiom
Hometown: Seattle, Washington
Height: 6' 1" **Weight:** 192 lbs
Eyes: Brown **Hair:** None

Super capabilities: Super intelligence; able to shrink to the size of an atom; sunglasses give x-ray vision; lab coat allows for travel through time and space.

Origin: Since birth, Max Axiom seemed destined for greatness. His mother, a marine biologist, taught her son about the mysteries of the sea. His father, a nuclear physicist and volunteer park ranger, schooled Max on the wonders of earth and sky.

One day on a wilderness hike, a megacharged lightning bolt struck Max with blinding fury. When he awoke, Max discovered a newfound energy and set out to learn as much about science as possible. He traveled the globe earning degrees in every aspect of the field. Upon his return, he was ready to share his knowledge and new identity with the world. He had become Max Axiom, Super Scientist.

GLOSSARY

continental drift (KON-tuh-nuhn-tuhl DRIFT) — the slow movement of the earth's continents

core (KOR) — the inner part of earth that is made of solid and molten metal

crust (KRUHST) — the outer layer of earth; the crust is made of lighter-weight rocks.

detect (di-TEKT) — to notice or discover something

epicenter (EP-uh-sent-ur) — the point on the earth's surface directly above the place where an earthquake occurs

fault (FAWLT) — a crack in earth's crust where two plates meet

fracture (FRAK-chur) — a break or crack in something

magnitude (MAG-nuh-tood) — a measure of the amount of energy released by an earthquake

mantle (MAN-tuhl) — the layer of hot, dense rock that surrounds earth's core

plate (PLAYT) — a large sheet of rock that is a piece of earth's crust

predict (pri-DIKT) — to say what you think will happen in the future

rupture (ruhp-chur) — to break open or to burst

seismic (SIZE-mik) — something that is caused by or related to an earthquake

seismogram (SIZE-muh-grahm) — the written record of an earthquake

tsunami (tsoo-NAH-mee) — a large, destructive wave caused by an underwater earthquake

volcanic eruption (vol-KAN-ik e-RUHPT-shuhn) — the action of throwing out rock, hot ash, or lava with great force

READ MORE

Armentrout, David, and Patricia Armentrout. *Earthquakes.* Earth's Power. Vero Beach, Fla.: Rourke, 2007.

Burgan, Michael. *The Great San Francisco Earthquake and Fire.* Disasters in History. Mankato, Minn.: Capstone Press, 2008.

Rae, Alison. *Earthquakes and Volcanoes.* Looking at Landscapes. North Mankato, Minn.: Smart Apple Media, 2006.

Simon, Seymour. *Earthquakes.* Washington, D.C.: Smithsonian, 2006.

Thoron, Joe. *Earthquakes.* Kaleidoscope. New York: Marshall Cavendish Benchmark, 2007.

Walker, Niki. *Tsunami Alert!* Disaster Alert! New York: Crabtree, 2006.

INTERNET SITES

FactHound offers a safe, fun way to find Internet sites related to this book. All of the sites on FactHound have been researched by our staff.

Here's how:
1. Visit *www.facthound.com*
2. Choose your grade level.
3. Type in this book ID **1429613289** for age-appropriate sites. You may also browse subjects by clicking on letters, or by clicking on pictures and words.
4. Click on the **Fetch It** button.

FactHound will fetch the best sites for you!

INDEX